Effective Church Committee

A Member's Handbook

Louis A. Towson

Resource Publications, Inc.
San Jose, California

Reprint Department
Resource Publications, Inc.
160 E. Virginia Street #290
San Jose, CA 95112-5876
1-408-286-8505 (voice)
1-408-287-8748 (fax)

Library of Congress Cataloging-in-Publication Data

Towson, Louis A,. 1947–
   The effective church committee: a member's handbook /
Louis A. Towson.
    p. cm.
   ISBN 0-89390-479-1
   1. Church meetings. 2. Church committees. I. Title.
BV652.15.T69 2000
254'.6--dc21   99-058938

Printed in the United States of America

04 03 02 01 00 | 5 4 3 2 1

Editorial director: Nick Wagner
Production coordinator: Mike Sagara
Copyeditor: Robin Witkin

Contents

Chapter One

Now That You've Been Asked ...

If someone has asked you to serve on a parish committee or group you might be pondering several questions, the chief one being, *Do I really want to get involved?*

For most of us the church is a place to worship and learn. We go on Sunday and at other times to hear good preaching, celebrate our faith in worship, and maybe take a class. But the church does much more. Prayer groups, parish dinners, retreats, and festivals abound. Youth ministry often takes a large share of parish resources. Ministry to the elderly, sick, and homebound also requires a lot of time and energy. Churches help the less fortunate with food, housing, medical care, and advocacy. They reach out to the unchurched with the message of Jesus Christ. Caring for buildings and grounds and managing financial and legal matters requires constant attention, too.

People like you are needed to serve on elected boards and energize parish organizations and committees. Is it worth taking the next step, especially if it means a greater demand on your time and energy?

"I want my church to lift me up spiritually," some say, "If I take a job, I will probably be over there at odd times haggling about money or debating about what color to paint the nursery. Where's the spirituality in that?" True, it is one thing to sit next to people in worship, but quite another to sit with them in a group that is wrestling with a knotty problem. In the first case not much is demanded, unless they sing off-key or fidget. You can always sit somewhere else next time. In the second, though, you might be on opposite sides of a question and have your patience tested to the breaking point.

Scripture warns us about the danger of segregating worldly concerns from holiness. In Jesus, God entered human flesh. During his travels he saw everyday challenges as opportunities for the glory of heaven to shine, evoke faith, and transform unlikely people. Crossing a lake in a storm-tossed boat, facing the task of feeding a multitude with meager provisions, and even attending a wedding party where the wine ran out provided chances for God's love and power to blossom. Spiritual growth does not come only through worship or study but by lifting common tasks up to serve God's purpose.

Let's suppose we go backstage after attending a play. We will find a score of people unseen by the audience who handled sound effects, adjusted lighting, and assembled scenery to create settings for the players. Those realistic trees in the forest scene were painstakingly crafted from papier-mâché. The actress who portrayed the sprightly young girl now sits exhausted in her dressing room, soaking her feet.

What met our eyes and ears was a moving drama that touched our hearts, yet behind it lay years of training, months of preparation, and an army of dedicated people working to tell the story.

In the same way, Sunday worship lifts up the truth of the Gospel. Behind it lies writing the sermon, choir rehearsal, preparing the bulletin, arranging the flowers, polishing, and cleaning. When we arrive for the service, does a well-kept yard greet us? Who did the cutting and trimming? Who wrote the check for the electricity that illumines the building, powers the organ, and controls the temperature? There's a new family sitting in the third row because last Tuesday one of your members saw the moving van arrive and stopped in to invite them to church. Who visits the sick and prays daily for them? We petition the Lord for social justice, but who serves in the soup kitchen or volunteers in the clinic?

The Author of Life needs a production company to enact the saving story. All we do flows into and out of worship. It is a signal event in which everything finds purpose and direction as it's offered to God. Becoming involved in the inner workings of ministry does not hamper our spirituality but deepens it.

Difficulties do arise. We have heard people say, "I've had my feelings hurt," or "Church politics gets vicious!" Because its aim is high, its failings are more obvious than those of other institutions. That simply means that we have to deal with people realistically, knowing that inside we're all a bit like turtles with hard shells over our hearts. If we have come to faith in Jesus Christ, we should be equally realistic about God's grace. The shell has been broken. Alienation from God doesn't have to be the last word. As surely as Christ rose from the grave, we can be forgiven our wrongs and have power to forgive others. It is part of picking up our cross and following Christ, and it will make the winding path we travel a way of blessing.

A project's success never lies merely in getting something done. It is linked with what happens to the team on the way to its completion. With everyone paying attention to Jesus, who is always present where two or three or a dozen committee members gather, a group can overcome differences, surmount obstacles, and accomplish something significant for others, often with a unity that's a joy to experience.

Is involvement really worth it? To answer that, we have to go into the innermost places of our hearts and pose the question a little differently: *Am I being called through God's church to deeper awareness and more faithful response to his limitless and loving work with me?*

Once we move beyond that question, another arises, *Can I do it?* I heard of a man who had been called to serve as lay leader for a weekend religious conference. It was a big responsibility, and he grappled with doubts about his worthiness and ability to fulfill the required tasks. "I'm not going to do it unless God gives me a concrete sign that he wants me to," he announced to his wife. The following week he was driving to another town over a stretch of road he'd never traveled before. As he passed a church these words leaped out at him: "God doesn't call those who are equipped; he equips those whom he calls." They were inscribed on a concrete sign.

It's often easy to sell ourselves short when assessing our abilities. Usually it's not highly specialized skills that are needed—just a willingness to let your gifts blend harmoniously with those of others. If you function smoothly in your occupation, you can be useful in your church as well. Self-doubt is humility. Pride is being sure that even God can't use you for any good purpose. Faith is the belief there's no limit to what God can do through you.

Next, examine your commitments. *Can I make the meetings? Will I have time to do the required work? Will I need to adjust my schedule?* Ask for a detailed job description. Get a definite picture of the demands and put yourself realistically into it.

After due consideration, the yes or no is up to you. Pray hard, reflect on Scripture. In Exodus 3 note Moses' reluctance to undertake the mission the Lord called him to. Let God's promise, "I will be with you," bring assurance that a child of God is never alone.

I'm tempted to pass on what a minister friend of mine always told those he invited to do a big job: "Pray hard about it; then say 'Yes!'"

Chapter Two

Defining Our Terms

Two Kinds of Committees

The two major kinds of committees are *standing* and *ad hoc*. A standing committee, sometimes called a commission, continues in existence from year to year and usually tends to a major area of business. Finance and buildings and grounds are examples. Their work is commonly specified in the by-laws. If not, their duties should be described in writing, adopted by the leadership, and reviewed from time to time.

An ad hoc committee forms to do a specific job and dissolves when it's done, for example, a group chosen to put on a church picnic or renovate the kitchen. That its life is temporary does not diminish the need for clear directives.

Other Important Terms

- *Authority* is the permission to act. Every organization has a structure that grants authority to individuals and groups in various ways. In most churches the clergy and the board are at the top, though the specific ways their powers are delineated vary. Committees are formed at the behest of a person or body in authority. Knowing who does what in your church's chain of command is a necessity.

- *Responsibility* is being answerable for any actions taken. The body that requests a committee's formation doesn't relinquish responsibility when the group is assembled. It delegates authority but holds on to responsibility. It is up to the committee leader to see that everything the group does is in accordance with that body's wishes.

- *Accountability* is faithfulness in the relationship. The committee and the authority above it are mutually accountable to each other, underlining the need for good communication more than anything else.

How It All Works

Let's say that a matter is brought to the church board's attention: people are complaining that they cannot hear very well in church. Because it has many issues to deal with, the board decides to appoint an ad hoc committee to look into the problem. Jack Grayson is the board member who chairs buildings and grounds, a standing committee, and is given the authority to select a chairperson and to see that a committee is formed to tackle the problem.

He asks Emily Peters who agrees to the assignment. She has no trouble gathering six people interested in solving the problem and begins meeting with them. Jack attends the first meeting because he's genuinely interested in the issue and wants firsthand experience of what the committee is doing to address it.

They outline several possibilities: poor acoustics, the need for a sound system, or simply the need for better use of voice by the readers and clergy. As they explore these areas over several meetings, Emily maintains her accountability to Jack by telling him what they are doing. Jack in turn reports to the board. That's his accountability.

At length the committee determines that a new sound system is in order. They research the cost by having several firms come by and look at the church. The committee has authority to ask for bids but not to commit the church to purchasing a sound system. Only the board can do that. It has the overall responsibility for the problem and the authority to commit the church to a course of action that requires church funds.

Emily submits a report and a recommendation as to which system the church should choose, thus completing her task and the committee's. Because Jack has been fully informed by her committee all along the way, he submits the report and recommendation to the board and answers all questions satisfactorily. The board approves the recommendation, allocates the money, and thanks Jack, Emily, and the committee for their hard work.

At this point the board will probably ask Jack to see to the installation of the system. He may ask Emily's committee to do so, but this is over and above what they were originally asked to do. However, having gained an enthusiasm for seeing a new system installed, they might jump at the chance. Jack has the authority also to get someone else to oversee it, or simply to do it himself.

Everyone involved acted freely in accordance with the authority they were rightfully accorded. Accountability was respected and responsibilities fulfilled. In addition, by going to meetings, Jack appropriately acted as what is called an *ex officio* member, taking part in the committee's activities to show his concern for their progress and to support their work but doing so without usurping the leadership of the chairperson.

The role of good communication was paramount on all levels throughout the process, beginning with the board member who brought up a concern voiced by people in the parish. A clear statement of what the actual task was flowed from the board down to the committee without confusion. Likewise, news of the group's activities was shared with all concerned.

Chapter Three

The Unspoken Covenant

When God made a covenant with the Hebrews, he told Moses to cut two stone tablets and take them up on Mount Sinai where he would inscribe the Ten Commandments. He wanted to make the conditions of the covenant clear to all.

A committee lives by a covenant, too, but its conditions are often unspoken. We tend to feel that others should simply understand what we expect of them and that it would spoil things if we told them outright. So we don't, and when they fail to adhere to our secret hopes, we feel let down.

Throwing subtlety to the wind, I offer the following as a set of working principles for all committees. If any of them are breached, an apology and corrective action are in order.

A leader expects those who serve to

1. Be on time for meetings and remain until adjournment

2. Listen

3. Contribute ideas, and be flexible enough to modify those ideas as a group vision or plan evolves

4. Do the tasks required on time and according to the specifications of the group or leader

5. Keep the leader informed about progress on assigned tasks as well as any difficulties that hinder their completion

6. Approach the whole enterprise with Christian love for all who will be involved in or affected by the committee's work

7. Respect confidentiality

8. Lift the committee's work in prayer regularly

The committee member expects the leader to

1. Be on time, if not early, for all meetings

2. Be prepared for the meetings and reasonably organized about the committee's work

3. Run the meetings so that all business gets done without wasted effort and with due consideration for persons attending

4. Provide all pertinent information to the members in a timely fashion

5. Coordinate the work with other bodies in the parish to avoid overlap, encroachment, or misunderstanding

6. Ensure that all the committee's work is done with the approval of the authority structure

7. Respect confidentiality

8. Lift the committee's work up in prayer regularly

Meetings

People can show each other consideration by arriving on time. Surroundings should be conducive to good work. Someone might come early to adjust the thermostat, make coffee, and set up the room.

The meeting has two main functions: information exchange and decision making. A good leader prepares a written agenda listing the ground to be covered. It's best to make reports in writing with copies for everyone. They provide details that may be missed in oral transmission or later forgotten.

It is everyone's responsibility to stick to the topic at hand. Meandering from one subject to another wastes time. Don't be offended if the leader nudges everyone back on track when discussion wanders.

Assigned Tasks

Action follows decision. Make sure you know what you're to do and by when. Report your progress to the leader regularly so that your work can be coordinated with that of others.

Be aware of the human tendency to procrastinate. Try to get the job done well before the deadline in case something unexpected arises.

Church Unity

No parish group is an island unto itself. All members should see themselves as part of the whole and avoid needless friction or competition with others.

Under Authority

The ordained leader and the church board are responsible for all you do. They want you to be successful. But there may be times when they pull on the reins or request an alternate course of action because of considerations beyond the ken of your group.

Pastoral Care

In recent years much has been discovered about the spiritual power of small groups to enhance the mission of the church. Both the leader and participants should recognize the necessity of developing a community that's centered on Christ. There are many ways to enhance a sense of family. Take some time to get to know each other. Have an occasional meal together or specify part of a meeting for personal sharing. Humor relaxes and even heals. Good planning that creates an easy flow of ideas minimizes anxiety.

There are those who naturally enjoy building relationships while others want to stay firmly "on task" without diversions. Both types need to be ministered to—the former to understand there's a definite job to do, the latter to realize that drawing closer to God and caring for each other will enhance the group's success.

Confidentiality

We should be clear about what deserves to be confidential and what doesn't. A primary principle is that a church should never be allowed to become riddled with secrets. Like hastily dug tunnels beneath a field, covert operations will undermine its common life. Important information, especially about how money has been or will be spent, needs to be shared with everyone.

Keeping track of money contributions week by week or how much individuals are pledging is another matter. Confidentiality in these cases involves keeping a sacred trust that is as profound as the priest's confessional.

Some clarification may be needed about other matters. Mentioning things about oneself or someone else that are of a personal, confessional nature and not to be repeated is an unfair burden to place on people in any group, especially one brought together for a church project. That kind of information, which may be deeply disturbing to some, should be shared only with the most trusted confessor, confidant, or support group.

At other times problems simply arise from friction between one or more members. People say and do things they shouldn't have and wouldn't have if they had not become so upset. In cases like these confidentiality falls more under the heading of not spreading gossip and ill feeling within the parish family, a responsibility whose value cannot be minimized.

In any case, it's no fair for anyone who has been taken into confidence to go to an outsider with a "Promise not to tell?" That's tacit permission to spread the word to what can become a veritable network of others who all promise not to tell either.

Prayer

Sometimes we hear that the church should be run more like a business. We often oblige too readily by leaving faith at the door. Begin and end your meeting with prayer and ask continuously for the Holy Spirit to empower every phase of your work. Who knows? The little "coincidences" that fall into a pattern of success might inspire business folks among you to conduct their affairs more like a church.

Chapter Four

Getting Specific: Purpose, Vision, Goals, and Objectives

Purpose

Instead of being like the man who closed his eyes and tossed a ball over his shoulder claiming that the place it landed was his target, your committee will work best if it chooses its mark and takes careful aim.

Although it may be doing many tasks, your committee has one central purpose. Before anything begins it's essential to know it. If you and your chairperson are unclear and too much of your purpose is clouded by assumptions, meet with the right parish leader and clarify it. Know thy purpose.

Vision

Capturing a vision of where you want to go is the first step in moving forward with *enthusiasm,* a term that means "to be filled with God." Read Isaiah 6, in which a transcendent vision of God fills the prophet's heart and mind, grants him forgiveness, calls him to a noble task, and empowers him to accomplish it. Without such a vision, what direction would his life have taken?

Vision is a gift of God, which we have to be open to receive. Isaiah sought the devotional atmosphere of the temple to heighten his receptiveness. Taking quiet moments to contemplate the tasks before us can infuse a pedestrian job with spiritual depth and power.

Make a picture. Ask yourself, "When the work is done what do I see? hear? What does it feel like?" Include the physical location and specific people. Try with all the resources of your imagination to bring it into sharp focus. Offer it to God in prayer. Does it seem right to the Holy Spirit and to your group? Once attained and held aloft, this vision will inspire your efforts and provide refreshment when the going gets difficult.

Goals and Objectives

Once the vision is in place, what do you do next? This is where the value of goals and objectives becomes evident. They provide answers to the questions *who, what, where, when,* and *how.*

The vision you have conceived may be expressed in words and phrases that are metaphorical, artistic, or even poetic. A goal, on the other hand, is a brief, businesslike description of the concrete product or specific action that will result. It's always realistic, measurable, specific, and time bound.

For instance, on May 1 your group is assigned the task of finding a way to make newcomers feel welcome. Your goal might read: "To plan and implement a newcomer hospitality program by September 1." Both *plan* and *implement* are words that denote concrete action. *Newcomer hospitality program* accurately names the specific task you're tackling and the product that will result. *September 1* provides the time frame.

You may also include other information like cost or the name of a specific person or group that will be affected by your goal especially if it's for people other than your church family: "The Church Men's Group will provide a party for the residents of Sunshine Ranch children's home on December 23, at a cost of $200."

Once the goal is in place and preferably written down clearly, you need to outline the intermediate steps that will lead to accomplishing the goal. When put into writing, these objectives have the same structure as goals. The new member incorporation group may have several:

- To research church literature and interview leaders of other churches for methods of new member incorporation by June 1

- In light of that research, to design a process of new member incorporation appropriate for our own congregation and have it approved by the parish leadership by July 1

- To implement the program on September 1 by producing printed materials, recruiting and training volunteers, and planning events to take place in the coming year

Goals and objectives focus on what's ahead and help us focus energy and budget time, but they don't predetermine the future. Unexpected factors — sickness, schedule changes, even weather — can make us change our plans. Always have an itinerary, but be ready to make adjustments to it as the journey unfolds.

Action Plan

Because a committee functions best with each person fully engaged in its work, an action plan is helpful in outlining individual tasks. To create an action plan, simply place column headings at the top of a piece of paper as follows: Subject, Action, By Whom, By When, Cost.

Using the example of the newcomer hospitality committee again, we might construct the action plan as follows:

Subject	Action	By Whom	By When	Cost
Research	Check out and read resources in church library.	John Smith Bill Jones	June 1	0
	Prepare a report for the committee.			
	Inquire at local bookstores; purchase helpful books.	Mary Wilson Jane Allen	June 1	Up to $50
	Prepare a report for the committee.			
	Interview local church leaders.	Mary Clark Sam Billings	June 1	0
	Prepare a report for the committee.			

Later, as work progresses, it may begin to look like this:

Subject	Action	By Whom	By When	Cost
Printed Materials	Design newcomers' brochure.	Mary Clark	Aug. 15	0
	Submit to committee for approval.			
Recruitment	Design greeter training program.	Bill Jones Sam Billings Jane Adams	Aug. 1	0
	Submit to committee for approval.			
Events	Consult with church office to schedule newcomer dinners.	John Smith	Aug. 15	0

The action plan provides not only a way for the leader to coordinate activities but helps everyone literally stay on the same page. It enhances the group's cooperation and sense of community.

The very task of committing goals, objectives, and action plans to paper brings a mental clarity all its own. To serve their purpose, they must be written down and given to each member.

For some the temptation will be to become too detailed—*Members meet at the church for car pool at 7:00 P.M.; assemble in designated vehicles by 7:03 P.M.; embark for the auditorium by 7:05 P.M.* The watchwords are *specific* and *simple*. Strive for conciseness and write down only the major actions you are to take.

Chapter Five

A Creative Approach

God has given us supple minds to use in imaginative ways. Church work calcifies when we constantly revert back to the old formulas. "Sing to the Lord a new song!" the psalmist tells us. If creative efforts are lifted to God in love, we can grow in marvelous ways. Although we often equate the creative process with art, it's a gift to use any time there's a problem to solve.

The first step is to formulate a question to get our ideas flowing and challenge us to see ourselves and the world in a different light. God's questions to Job help him see truth more clearly than the answers of his friends. We still ponder the words of the angel outside Christ's empty tomb, "Why look among the dead for one who is alive?"

Questions mobilize our inventiveness. As children we did it all the time. *How can I make a hut quickly in my backyard?* Overturned lawn chairs covered with a bedspread became the outlaw hideout. *How could lunchtime at school be a little more fun?* Combine ice cream and milk to make a chocolate shake. A committee may ask, *How can we plan a church picnic for all ages to enjoy?*

Two or more ideas placed side by side energize each other — hard edges dissolve letting the contents intermingle so that new notions will be born.

Initially committees need to find a way of silencing the inner critic to liberate the imagination. Perhaps the group planning the picnic should first have each member come up with the wildest idea possible, just to get the ball rolling.

"I want everyone to fly!" someone says.

"Let's pan for gold!"

"Serve buffalo meat!"

Good! Write each one down. The task right now isn't to present sensible ideas but to break loose from conventional patterns. With crazy notions on the newsprint, other ideas begin to emerge as the group reflects.

"Buffalo makes me think of animals. How about having the picnic near a petting zoo or providing pony rides for the kids?"

"Panning for gold reminds me of the Wild West. Maybe we could have a cowboy theme."

"Flying reminds me of balloons, kites, and paper airplanes."

As committee members begin to reflect on how they want to accommodate a wide range of age groups, other ideas emerge.

"Maybe we could pair up a child with an older person to fly a kite."

"Let's offer a ride to the people who don't drive."

The ideas fly and they're all put down. For now the group has sidestepped questions like *Will that really work? How much will it cost? Who can we get to do it?* in favor of enjoying the broad horizon.

After enough time has been given to the "blue sky" approach, and a period of silent reflection allowed, more practical elements can be introduced. Perhaps buffalo meat wouldn't evoke enthusiasm from the congregation, but changing from burgers and hot dogs to barbecued chicken would. Instead of only volleyball and baseball, provide kites along with a quiet activity like bingo for young and old alike. The group is on its way to planning a day full of both the familiar and the new that everyone will enjoy because they chose to move out of the ruts.

Because making something new often involves unmaking something that existed before, creative efforts might meet with resistance. The child's mother may frown on having her prized bedspread used to make a playhouse. The teacher may call down those who play with their milk and ice cream. As irrational as it may sound, having chicken instead of burgers and hot dogs might strike many as violating some long-standing sacred principle — "We've never done it that way before!"

Courage and boldness are traits common to creative people. But unlike most artists, church workers operate in a community setting in which tradition, custom, and peoples' feelings can't be callously ignored. Things are done to build up the body. Being courageous in presenting something new means being courteous enough to explain it fully, to persuade gently, and to modify a plan for a valid reason. It's not attempting to please everyone but doing what is best for the community that is paramount.

We often decry our limitations. Budget, attitudes, and a host of other constraints can make us feel pinched. But creativity thrives in a well-contained environment. A shortage of resources prods us to make the most of what we have.

Creativity is more than just a technique. It is a way of life and spills over delightfully into other roles we play. Sharpening our minds today on a church problem prepares us to solve a work dilemma tomorrow. It even seems to be a gift of God that we can work out answers unconsciously. After some intense thought, give the brain a rest. Don't be surprised if you're crying out "Eureka!" in the middle of weeding the garden or on a drive to the grocery as the answer emerges full-blown from nowhere.

"Blessed are those who have not seen and yet believe," Jesus said to Thomas and the other disciples after the resurrection. Faith rests in imaginative power more than we often admit. To look to the future and see something good coming out of bad requires the creative hopefulness God bestows through his grace.

Perhaps being a Christian is indeed to be more of an artist than we realize. We take the seen and unseen resources God has given us, and by the means he has provided, fashion something good and true from them, to embody our thankfulness and reflect his glory.

Chapter Six

Making Decisions

The primary purpose for meeting together is two-fold: to share information and to make decisions. Although a committee does not have to follow Robert's Rules of Order strictly, there's wisdom in its meeting structure. All pertinent information is reported to everyone first, and then decisions are made afterward under old and new business.

It may seem sensible at times to do otherwise. Why not make decisions immediately as they unfold in the course of reporting? Let's suppose that a committee charged with redecorating the church living room has just been told that a furniture store owner has offered them their choice between two couches he plans to give away. They are both quite different in color and style. Which one do they choose? If they try to decide now, information from other people who haven't reported yet is not available. To make the best choice, they need to hear what the options are for wall and floor coverings, curtains, lighting, and other furniture.

The best practice is to put out all the information first and list the decisions each report calls for.

When all reports are in, go down the list and tackle each decision in turn. This process maintains the integrity of each report, keeps the group on one subject at a time, and ensures that every decision will be fully informed.

Discussion, Decision, And Conflict

Decisions involve discussion, which is an attempt to gain a complete understanding of all the issues surrounding options before the group. In forming the whole picture, everyone's viewpoint is vital and listening to each other is paramount.

Discussion isn't mere conversation. Its purpose is to lead the group to take concrete action. Informality helps members feel relaxed and at home together, but it should not be a license to stray from the subject. Although staying on track is everyone's job, the leader's task is to make sure they do and manage the discussion so that everyone is heard and a decision is reached in a reasonable amount of time.

Decisions should be written down clearly and noted in the meeting report or minutes, but making formal motions and tabulating votes should be unnecessary. A group should strive for consensus and unanimity. After all, if the committee is not united in its major decisions, how can it begin to commend them to the rest of the congregation? This raises the question of what to do when conflict enters unannounced.

Conflict is a natural occurrence and need not be a bad thing. People tend to avoid or deny conflict because it can cast a long shadow of fear and ill feeling over a group if it is not handled well. It's like a dark forest a band of travelers is moving through. The thick foliage tends to divide some members into groups and isolate others, threatening everyone's successful arrival at the clearing beyond.

Three things should be kept in mind. *Prayer* and seeking the guidance Christ offers unites people's hearts in the mysterious and empowering love of the Holy Spirit. The *goal*, like a light beckoning on the other side of the trees, reminds everyone of the group's high purpose to better the lives of others. *Communication* ensures that the group will remain connected. To keep listening is to honor the tie that binds.

A committee does not have the luxury of debating something forever, but needs to act within a set time frame. Every effort should be made to secure unanimity. If it can't be achieved, then a formal vote should be taken and recorded, with the minority point of view in the matter duly recognized, noted, and included in any report that is made to a higher authority.

Equally important as the goal is what happens to the group on the way to fulfilling it. Conflict is natural but need not lead to division. With prayer, a clear goal, and good communication, a group might be amazed to discover that conflict serves to deepen their mutual respect for each other and strengthen their sense of community.

Decisions calling for definite steps to be taken need to be acted on with dispatch. Each meeting should end with a summary of action items—who will be doing what and by when. Because procrastination is a specter that haunts many a committee, a month between meetings can be an eternity in which to forget information and assignments given at the previous one, especially when a large project is looming. But meeting frequently, written reminders, and a chairperson who is part bird dog when it comes to following up on assigned tasks cannot substitute for a committee member who simply does what he or she has promised to do in the time specified.

Chapter Seven

Your Committee Notebook

Organizing a notebook devoted solely to the work of the committee makes all aspects of your participation go smoother. Get some simple dividers and create the following sections:

Section I

- *Purpose:* Write the purpose statement assigned or decided on by your group on a single sheet of paper.

- *Vision:* Compose your personal vision statement. Include what you will see and hear at the completion of your work, describing your feelings of satisfaction for the success you will enjoy.

- *Goals and Objectives:* Write each goal at the top of a page with the accompanying objectives listed below it.

Section II

Agenda sheets, minutes, and your notes for each meeting go into this area. In this and the next two sections, it's more convenient to add new papers from back to front so the most recent material is always on top.

Section III

Action plan sheets may be placed here along with your personal lists of assignments and "to-do" items, ready to be checked off as things get done.

Section IV

Place all accumulated information in this section—reports, correspondence, and research data.

Section V

Include reference documents like a roster of names and addresses of committee members, board guidelines, church by-laws, or denominational rules in this section.

MOMS Ministry Resources

MOMS (Ministry of Mothers Sharing) is a rapidly growing ministry being organized around the country by mothers of all ages. Started by Paula Hagen, OSB, MOMS relies on a basic eight-session plan that helps mothers gather together, share stories, and become enriched spiritually. Typically, MOMS works as a springboard toward greater involvement in the parish.Order your risk-free evaluation kit today! The kit contains five key components: The MOMS Video, MOMS: Developing a Ministry, and MOMS: A Facilitator's Guide, MOMS: A Personal Journal.

MOMS Video

Paula Hagen
VHS, Approx. 18 min.

MOMS: A Personal Journal

Paula Hagen with Vickie LoPiccolo JennettPaper
144 pages, 7" x 10", 0-89390-508-9

MOMS: Developing a Ministry

Paula Hagen & Patricia Hoyt
Paper, 192 pages, 8.5" x 11", 0-89390-368-X

MOMS: A Facilitator's Guide

Paula Hagen, Vickie LoPiccolo Jennett, and Patricia Hoyt
Paper, 144 pages, 8.5" x 11", 0-89390-509-7

A Prayer Companion for MOMS

Vickie LoPiccolo Jennett with Paula Hagen
Paper, 104, 4" x 6", 0-89390-265-9

Resources for Grief Ministry

GRIEF MINISTRY: Helping Others Mourn

Donna Reilly Williams & JoAnn Sturzl

Paper, 195 pages, 5½" x 8½", 0-89390-233-0

GRIEF MINISTRY: Facilitator's Guide

JoAnn Sturzl & Donna Reilly Williams

Paper, 144 perforated pages, 8½" x 11", 0-89390-227-6

Grief Ministry: Helping Others Mourn combines spiritual and psychological insights about grief work. It covers general aspects of grieving, empathy, communication, listening, and prayer. The authors share insights on handling difficult situations, including such special cases as suicide, the death of a baby, job loss, AIDS, and divorce. The *Facilitator's Guide* shows how to set up a program to train grief ministers using *Grief Ministry: Helping Others Mourn* as a textbook. The guide includes group listening and role-playing exercises, scenarios for discussion, a resource listing, and useful photocopiable handouts.

COMPLICATED LOSSES, DIFFICULT DEATHS
A Practical Guide for Ministering to Grievers

Roslyn A. Karaban, PhD

Paper, 144 pages, 5½" x 8½", 0-89390-476-7

Suicide, sudden losses, lingering illnesses, the death of a child, murders, miscarriages and the like evoke grief symptoms and reactions that are more intense and last longer than "ordinary" grief. The author, a pastoral counselor, helps you understand complicated losses in your own life and prepares you to minister to others. Chapters cover types of complicated losses: ambiguous losses, losses with social stigmas, sudden losses, lingering losses, traumatic losses, violent losses, and untimely losses. A concluding section examines the need to care for caregivers. Intended for individual study or as a text for an advanced grief ministry course.

Resources for Youth Ministry

THREE-MINUTE DRAMAS FOR WORSHIP

Karen Patitucci

Paper, 261 pages, 5½" x 8½", 0-89390-143-1

Here are 72 easy-to-memorize skits perfect for your church, classroom, or prayer group. The Bible-based dramas include theme and Scripture references that will help you decide which ones best fit your particular needs. Also includes tips on how to write and direct your own short dramas.

THE SEVEN PRINCIPLES
OF EFFECTIVE YOUTH MINISTRY

Mark Springer and Cheryl Smith

Paper, 192 pages, 5½" x 8½", 0-89390-341-8

"Up to date without being trendy, God-centered without being impossible, the authors are offering us something that is both information and inspiration... this book will feed the passion."—Richard Rohr, OFM Center for Action and Contemplation.

YOUTH MINISTRY ACTIVITY BOOK
For Ages 11-14

Rose Thomas Stupak, IHM

Paper, 105 pages, 5½" x 8½", 0-89390-127-X

"The author offers a cafeteria of ideas that you can build on, according to your own situation. She provides you with the basic ingredients to structure your own pilgrimage, retreat, service project, dramatization, song, and pantomime for your specific group of teens."— Liguorian Magazine.

More Youth Ministry Resources

YOUTH PACKET

Edited by Wanda Scheuermann

Looseleaf, 8.5" x 11", September through August

The *Youth Packet* from CELEBRATING THE LECTIONARY (CTL) has everything you need to run lively youth sessions organized around the lectionary. Packets contain background materials, session plans, photocopiable handout masters, and other resource material. CELEBRATING THE LECTIONARY is a Roman Catholic liturgical catechesis program series for parishes and schools. There are other age group teacher packets available — seven in all — each coordinated around the same Sunday readings. You only need one packet per group because all the handouts are photocopiable, which makes CTL very economical. Ages 14-18

BUILDING SELF-ESTEEM
A Workbook for Teens

Jerome Trahey

Illustrated, Paper, 128 pages, 8½" x 11", 0-89390-231-4

This workbook gives teens practical, original exercises that can help them find out who they are, what they value, and where they are going with what they value. It uniquely helps them discover their innate goodness and worth in light of the Gospel. Bulk discounts available.

PEER HELPER'S POCKETBOOK

Joan Sturkie and Valerie Gibson

Paper, 104 pages, 4" x 7", 0-89390-237-3

Here is a small book that has proven helpful in both empowering and instructing students. Written for peer helpers/counselors on the junior and senior high school levels as well as college. Everything for effective peer support is included. (A Peer Helper's Training Course is also available)

Resources for Preaching and Teaching

STORY POWER!
Compelling Illustrations for Preaching and Teaching

James A. Feehan

Paper, 120 pages, 5½" x 8½", 0-89390-304-3

To really get your point across you've got to tell stories. Good ones. Short ones. Powerful ones. Stories that intrigue. Stories that fascinate. Stories that capture the imagination. And then — your stories have to hook your listeners to the gospel message. These anecdotes and quick story illustrations meet that challenge.

FOR GIVE
Stories of Reconciliation

Lou Ruoff

Paper, 120 pages, 5½" x 8½", 0-89390-198-9

In this collection of original stories, Lou Ruoff focuses on gospel reconciliation stories: The Prodigal Son, The Unforgiving Servant, Seventy-Times-Seven, and more. Great for homily ideas, for catechesis, or for Re-membering Church sessions.

SERMONS FOR SERMON HATERS

Andre Papineau

Paper, 144 pages, 5½" x 8½", 0-89390-229-2

It's a preacher's dream — to turn on the turned off. That's Andre Papineau's specialty. He's a preacher, a psychotherapist, and an actor. Use his techniques to break open the Gospel in ways that reach even the most jaded.

PARABLES OF CONVERSION
Homilies and Stories Based on the Lectionary

Lou Ruoff

Paper, 128 pages, 5½" x 8½", 0-89390-403-1

To make a point about conversion, look into *Parables of Conversion*. Some are narratives, others more poetic. Some are dialogue, others are reflections that occur only within one's heart of hearts. Some are fantasy, others help you experience what it is like to live in the gutter with the muck of humanity. But each tale relates a set of experiences that lead, through grace, to a moment of conversion. And each parable poses a spiritual question while remaining open-ended — the better to encourage discussion and reflection.

MOTIVATING YOUR PARISH TO CHANGE:
Concrete Leadership Strategies for Pastors, Administrators, and Lay Leaders

Rev. Dave Heney

Paper, 128 pages, 5½" x 8½", 433-3

Using Moses' effort to lead his people to the Promised Land as a model, Rev. Heney lays out concrete strategies for motivating people that can be applied to any parish by any person in a leadership role.

Order from your local bookseller, or contact:

RESOURCE Resource Publications, Inc.
160 E. Virginia Street #290
San Jose, CA 95112-5876
408-286-8505
408-287-8748 (fax)
888-273-7782 (toll free, 8-5 PT)
www.rpinet.com